WALLPAPER

LET US DIVE LIKE FISH

DEEP INTO A REALM

OF PATTERNS AND PRINTS

for
Henriette

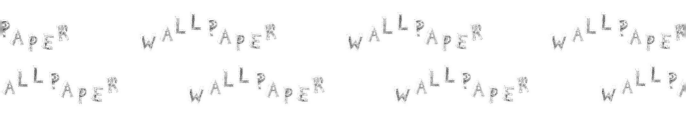

WALLPAPER

DECORATIVE ART

by
PHILIPPE MODEL

photography
MARIE-PIERRE MOREL

SCRIPTUM EDITIONS

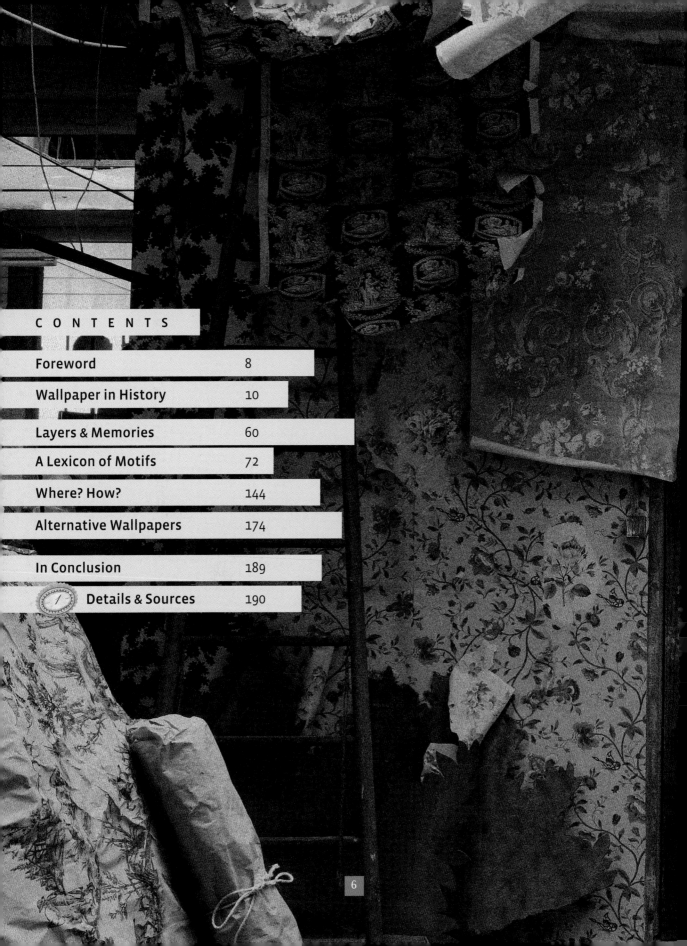

CONTENTS

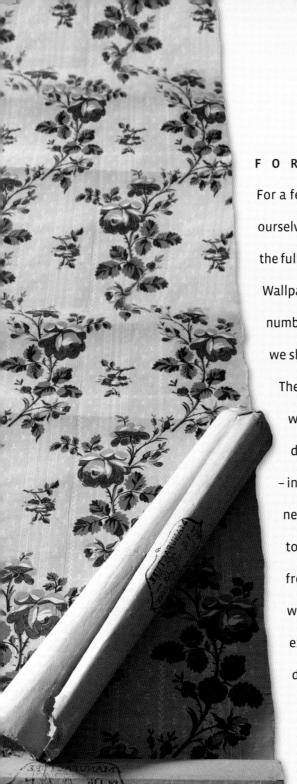

F O R E W O R D

For a few precious moments, let us indulge the pleasure of losing ourselves in the world of wallpaper, eyes wide open so as to savour to the full all that this world of fantasy and imagination and has to offer. Wallpaper has always set out to amaze. Like children counting the number of different images they can find in their bedroom wallpaper, we should be ever curious, ever alert.

Then we may begin to understand the ways in which wallpapers with their ever-changing patterns offer us not only their lavish displays of colour and harmony, but also – and more importantly – infinite scope for our own dreams and visions, responding to our needs for both harmony and poetry. In these pages I have set out, to present my own vision – chronological and thematic but far from exhaustive – of the astonishing decorative potential of wallpaper, both historically and today. Last but not least, the examples in these pages will I am sure demonstrate beyond doubt that wallpaper is good for our wellbeing!

PREVIOUS PAGES
On the dominotier's shelves: wallpapers by Brunschwig, Sandberg, Sanderson, Vinilia and Zuber.
LEFT
c.1785. Wallpaper with a repeat pattern of roses.
OPPOSITE
A few of the innumerable volumes in the Zuber archives.

WALLPAPER IN

HISTORY

With Gutenberg and the development of the printing press in 1440, a new world opened up. Text was rapidly liberated, with images soon following in its wake. Prints and engravings were reproduced in large numbers, and someone had the idea of using woodblock engravings to print simple patterns on paper, then gluing these edge to edge to decorate alcoves, niches and bed ends. These decorative sheets were known as dominos. Once established, the technique altered little: provincial dominos from the second half of the eighteenth century barely differ from those of previous centuries. Meanwhile the appearance of new and much more sophisticated techniques paved the way for the development of wallpaper as we know it today. Dominos would now be relegated to lining drawers, chests and armoires.

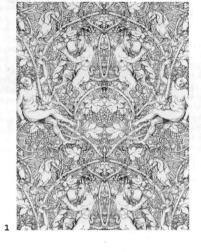

1

2

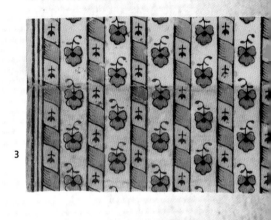

3

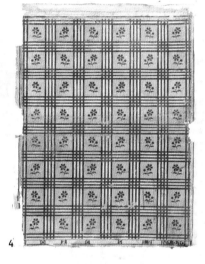

4

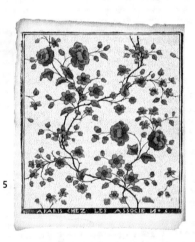

5

6

1 : The earliest surviving
example is German and
dates from 1525.
2–8 : French provincial
dominos from the 1760s,
from the towns of Blois,
Chartres, Nantes, Orléans,
Rouen, Tours and Troyes.

7

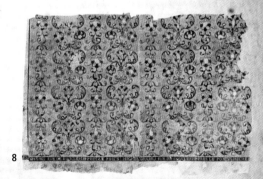

8

SECOND HALF OF THE 18TH CENTURY

1765-1775 FROM WALLPAPER TO WAISTCOATS:
CHINESE TREES OF LIFE AND FLORAL MOTIFS

I MOUNTED THIS

REPRODUCTION OF A FRENCH

SCREEN IN A WOODEN FRAME

1775–1785. Neoclassicism is all the rage. The motifs, always centred and symmetrical, take their inspiration from Roman grotesques, but with startling touches of French whimsy – bees, dogs, cats, ribbons – amid the bouquets, garlands and ferns.

CENTRE : Reproduction of a screen of c.1785, Iksel.

c.1790. A skilful restoration of a geometrically patterned wallpaper and frieze.

BIZARRE GEOMETRICAL DESIGNS AND FANTASTICAL
EXOTICISM BEAR WITNESS TO THE UPHEAVALS
OF THE AGE OF REVOLUTION, 1785–1790.

1760–1805: SECOND HALF OF THE EIGHTEENTH CENTURY

The veritable craze for *l'art de vivre* and interior decoration that swept all levels of French society at this period was to lend tremendous impetus to the development of wallpaper manufacturing. Major technical advances now opened up almost limitless possibilities, and large specialist firms grew up in both Paris and Lyon. In fashionable circles, however, these new wallpapers were used only in rooms of secondary importance, such as bedrooms, boudoirs and closets, while wood panelling was preferred for the more important public and reception rooms. From 1760 to the end of the century, wave after wave of fashions succeeded each other. First of all, bouquets of dog roses, eglantines and pinks, garlands and latticework rubbed shoulders with chinoiseries, trees of life thronged with butterflies and birds, and bucolic tableaux in the manner of 'toile de Jouy'. Meanwhile the bourgeoisie adopted the grand style in the form of *tontisses*, or flock wallpapers: high-quality reproductions of the heavy damasks of Louis XIV's reign, with motifs applied with glue in *poussière de laine*. From 1775, the growing vogue for classical antiquity saw a return to the airy arabesques and grotesques that had graced the walls of the Palladian villas of the sixteenth century. These were followed by motifs drawn from the frescoes and decorative details of Pompeii, with columns, friezes, palmettes and symmetrical arrangements of cameos, medallions and classical figures. Already – in a development that was to become a defining feature of wallpaper's unique character – designs were produced in a range of fanciful alternatives, with patterns that were fragmented or eccentric. Geometrical and

OPPOSITE
1805.. Wallpaper panel with medallion and drapery by Percier & Fontaine. Upper frieze : **c.1790.**. Réveillon factory. Lower frieze : **1795.** Jacquemart & Bénard.

RIGHT
1 : **c.1810.** French Border.
2 and 3 : **c.1800.** French box.
4 : **1835.** Border, Dufour & Leroy.

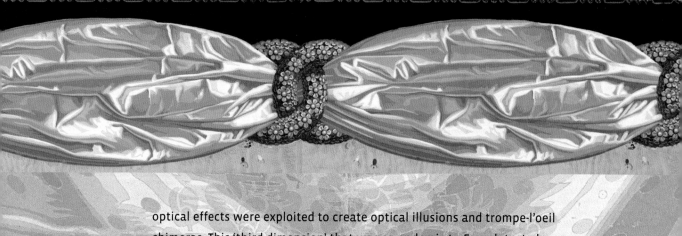

optical effects were exploited to create optical illusions and trompe-l'oeil chimeras. This 'third dimension' that was so endemic to French taste has remained an enduring presence in the wallpaper story. The colours used were also highly flamboyant. In comparison with mural paintings, wallpaper was so easy to apply that clients were tempted to try more risqué colour contrasts. Before 1760, backgrounds remained 'virgin', and were simply polished with agate. From around 1770 coloured backgrounds started to appear, deepening to the darkest tones in the 1790s before suddenly becoming vividly intense by the turn of the century.

FIRST HALF OF THE NINETEENTH CENTURY

Anyone with an interest in eighteenth-century wallpaper design will be struck by its similarities with fabric designs of the time. This was not so much a matter of imitation as of influence, since every motif then current – whether carved on panelling or chairs or embroidered on gentlemen's waistcoats – was the creation of the same artists and designers. In the early nineteenth century, wallpaper gradually began to throw off its inferiority complex as the poor relation of textiles, and instead began to imitate fabric designs, to take its inspiration from them, and even to outshine them. With wallpaper it was possible to deck out an entire salon in draperies, only more gracefully and artistically than would have been possible with even the choicest of fabrics. Heavy draperies no longer impinged on living space, the folds of their

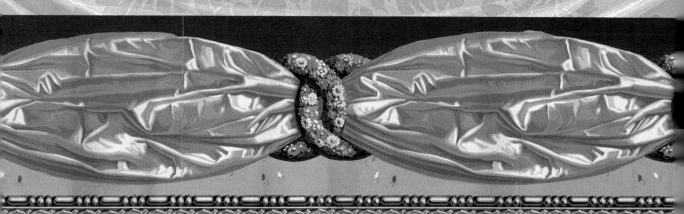

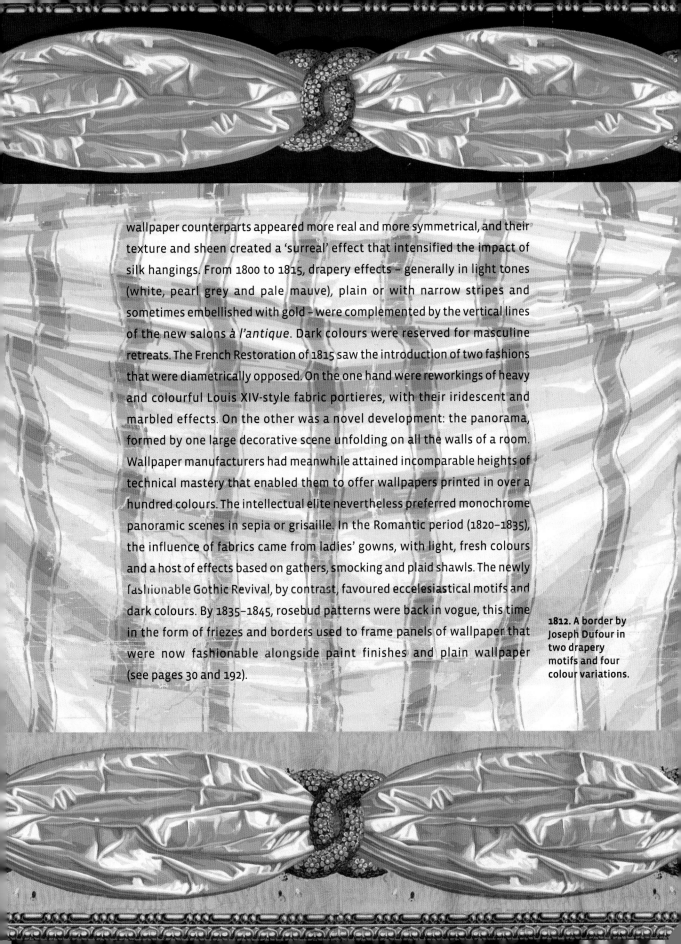

wallpaper counterparts appeared more real and more symmetrical, and their texture and sheen created a 'surreal' effect that intensified the impact of silk hangings. From 1800 to 1815, drapery effects – generally in light tones (white, pearl grey and pale mauve), plain or with narrow stripes and sometimes embellished with gold – were complemented by the vertical lines of the new salons *à l'antique*. Dark colours were reserved for masculine retreats. The French Restoration of 1815 saw the introduction of two fashions that were diametrically opposed. On the one hand were reworkings of heavy and colourful Louis XIV-style fabric portieres, with their iridescent and marbled effects. On the other was a novel development: the panorama, formed by one large decorative scene unfolding on all the walls of a room. Wallpaper manufacturers had meanwhile attained incomparable heights of technical mastery that enabled them to offer wallpapers printed in over a hundred colours. The intellectual elite nevertheless preferred monochrome panoramic scenes in sepia or grisaille. In the Romantic period (1820–1835), the influence of fabrics came from ladies' gowns, with light, fresh colours and a host of effects based on gathers, smocking and plaid shawls. The newly fashionable Gothic Revival, by contrast, favoured ecclesiastical motifs and dark colours. By 1835–1845, rosebud patterns were back in vogue, this time in the form of friezes and borders used to frame panels of wallpaper that were now fashionable alongside paint finishes and plain wallpaper (see pages 30 and 192).

1812. A border by Joseph Dufour in two drapery motifs and four colour variations.

1825-1835 REFRESHING ROMANTICISM

1835-1845

OPPOSITE This romantic décor mixes Mauny friezes by Zuber with distressed paintwork.
1 : c.1835. French Gothic motif. / 2 : 1838. Jules Desfossé. / 3 : 1789. Réveillon factory. / 4 : 1878. Coptic design in velveteen, Leroy.
RIGHT Frieze, 1840s.

1796

U331

1850-1860

33

Foliage and pheasants, after a period design, Nobilis.

c.1870. Embossed and polished faux leather wallpapers.

SECOND HALF OF THE NINETEENTH CENTURY

The Empress Eugénie (like her cousin Princess Mathilde) adored flowers, with a particular passion for generous, full-blown roses. Wallpapers smothered with roses, lilies and hydrangea blooms were created for these ladies, creating for them the illusion of being engulfed by lavish pergolas laden with trusses of deliciously perfumed flowers. Under the French Third Republic, after 1870, technical advances such as cylinder printing ensured that there was a wallpaper to suit every pocket. Now wallpaper – whether genuinely economical or deceptively so (the *grande bourgeoisie*, for instance, preferred it embossed and varnished to mimic Cordoba leather) – was ubiquitous, from the bedrooms immortalized by Bonnard in his paintings to government offices. Patterns were based on emblems, coats of arms or posies of three iris, tulips or crocuses in diagonal repeat patterns, and colours were invariably

c.1870. Leather wallpaper in a pattern of floral posies.

Pheasants on the study walls.

NEARLY THREE DECADES OF
warm and dark, with a high finish that verged on the glossy. For wealthy
DIAGONAL REPEAT PATTERNS
clients, or those who wished to appear so, the largest manufacturers
IN AUTUMNAL SHADES
continued the vogue for dark panoramic scenes featuring historical, chivalric

or exotic subjects. Amid a plethora of dubious offerings described as 'neo-

this' or 'in the style of that', wallpaper descended into its first period of

decadence. Eventually, around 1890, the first designers to specialize in the

field appeared in England, developing their own highly defined and

characteristic styles. Outstanding among them were William Morris,

Christopher Dresser and Walter Crane.

1870-1895

37

WILLIAM MORRIS, 1880

HECTOR GUIMARD, 1896

The early years of the twentieth century were illumined by the dazzling brilliance of Art Nouveau. Elongated, sinuous lines inspired by grasses and flag irises epitomized all the pliant grace of nature in stylized form. Reeds, waves and water lilies were depicted in high relief, carved in polished wood. Frederick Walton invented Lincrusta, a wallpaper made from canvas covered with a gel made from linseed oil and wood flour that lent itself to deeply embossed patterns based on plant motifs. Deep friezes laden with interlaced designs of poppies, iris, waterlilies, peacock feathers, grasshoppers and scarabs were all the rage. The aftermath of the First World War saw a popular, spontaneous impulse to brighten up other living spaces, such as the kitchens, studies and passages of country homes, where decorators' clients were now keen to live and entertain in less formal settings. The following two decades saw the appearance of a multitude of cheerful wallpapers and friezes in geometric patterns. Daisies, convolvulus, stylized dahlias, fruit, birds and friendly animals appeared in kitchens, while bedrooms and boudoirs became bowers filled with armfuls of broom in vases, cascades of wisteria and fuchsia, clouds of cherry blossom, trails of morning glory and clumps of hollyhocks.

1932 THE SPIRIT OF

JAPONISME

THIS POWERFUL

WALLPAPER DESIGN BY

EDOUARD BENEDICTUS

HAS ALL THE IMPRESSIVE

FORCE OF A PAINTING

In the years 1920–1925, responding to demands from a cultured and well-informed clientele for more intellectual and artistic motifs, wallpaper manufacturers turned to famous artists with distinctive styles. Braque, Matisse and Dufy, among others, were invited to give their visions expressions in the form of modern wallpaper. The publisher Andrés Groult, himself a designer, commissioned Georges Barbier and Andrew Carnegie. The first Cubist designs, meanwhile, were produced by the artist Edouard Benedictus as early as 1915.

PREVIOUS PAGES
1932. Sample designs and decors from the Follot catalogue of 1932.

OPPOSITE
c.1920. Contrasting stripes and Cubist-inspired flowers by Edouard Benedictus.

RIGHT
1 : c. 1920. Jean Laboureur for Andrés Groult.
2 and 4 : 1927. Two designs by Edouard Benedictus.
3 : c.1920. Georges Barbier for Groult.

INTERPRETATIONS OF GARDEN
FLOWERS OWING NOTHING
TO NATURE IN EITHER
FORM OR COLOUR

OPPOSITE
Three swatches, c1925.
On the wall, foxgloves by
Suzy Hoodless for Osborne & Little.

ABOVE
1928. Characteristically geometric roses
with 'saddle stitch' effect, Charles Follot.

48

A '1940s SURREALIST'-INSPIRED ENSEMBLE
IN THE FACTORY, FEATURING CRABS,
LOBSTERS AND WALLPAPERS BY NOBILIS

1950s COLOURS, CINEMA

AND COMIC STRIPS

BELOW AND OPPOSITE
Two wallpapers from 1965, American (green
and yellow) and French (blue and pink).

CENTRE
1966. Flowered wallpaper by Cole & Son.

THE 1940s AND 1950s

In the years before the Second World War, patterns became simpler and
plain backgrounds were back in vogue, though now more definite and also
coloured (in misty blue, blotting-paper pink, baize green, brown, faded red).
Taking their cue from style guru Elsa Schiaparelli, the new pattern ranges
displayed a surrealist bias, mingling the conventional violets, bows and
feathers with fish and shellfish, sardine skeletons, gloves and shoes, lapdogs,
princesses and champagne bottles. Heraldic and wrought iron motifs were
arranged symmetrically on dark, plain or studded backgrounds. In the post-
war period, the 1950s offered a radically new palette of contemporary greys
and yellows, with splashes of brown, orange, duck-egg blue, red, beige and
black. Fantasy and imagination ruled in the choice of patterns, many inspired
by modern art. The paintings of Miró and contemporary vases and furniture
design inspired new motifs based on rounded forms such as the television,
boomerang and peanut. Etched with broken telephone lines, they make
reference to the work of numerous designers such as René Litt.

1975, DOMINOS: THE COMEBACK

The decade 1965–1975 opened with the explosive return of floral motifs – large, stylized and multicoloured. The English designer David Hicks brought the repeat geometric patterns of the earliest dominos back into fashion, enlarging them and colouring them in a palette of vivid turquoises, yellows, pinks, oranges and browns. Geometric designs became the ultimate in chic, supplanting even floral designs in the years 1975–1980. The following fifteen years were to see the decline of wallpaper in favour of flat planes of paintwork in a single colour. Around 1995 it returned to the spotlight in a novel and highly graphic way, with a new vogue for papering one wall – generally in a bold pattern and often with cut-outs – of minimalist loft spaces.

LEFT
1, 2, 3 and 4 : **1973**. Four characteristic designs by David Hicks.

OPPOSITE
A wallpaper designed by Ashley Hicks in the style of his father David for Cole & Son, interspersed with the square-and-circle collages that I love to make.

THE FUTURE WILL ALWAYS HOLD INFINITE

POSSIBILITIES FOR CREATING ELEGANT AND EXUBERANT

DECORS WITH WALLPAPER

CONTEMPORARY WALLPAPER

In late 2008, the Musée de la Publicité aux Arts Décoratifs in Paris staged an exhibition of the work of the designers Antoine & Manuel (see pages 56–57), so introducing a new public to wallpapers laden with ironic refernces to contemporary society and full of whimsy, combining motifs drawn from the world of computers, electronic circuit boards, dials and buildings under construction with paper hens and little monsters. A whole universe, in short, and a perfect expression of the poetic function of 'authentic' wallpaper. Presented in the upper galleries of the Louvre, these contemporary wallpapers and fabric wall coverings found themselves juxtaposed fortuitously with an Empire-era bee design. The two different generations complemented each other perfectly. Wallpaper comes full circle.

OPPOSITE
The grandiloquent gilding of the Louvre with Antoine & Manuel's tricolor meanders.

PREVIOUS PAGES
Wallpapers by Antoine & Manuel in the corridors of the Musée de la Publicité aux Arts Décoratifs.

RIGHT
1 : Bees by Farrow & Ball.
2 and 4 : Deux papiers Antoine & Manuel.
3 : Bees by Zuber.

LAYERS &
MEMORIES

An Art Deco wallpaper revealed under a more recent one.

Period blue pigments were of the finest quality.

OLD WALLPAPERS TELL
THEIR OWN TALES

I am not alone, I know, in responding to the tales that venerable wallpaper

has to tell. When I look up at an old building under demolition and see

shreds of wallpaper hanging from the exposed walls of what were once

rooms, or when I climb up into a dusty and abandoned attic, there to

discover one garret room after another, each with its own wallpaper, I am

transported to another world. Every wallpaper tells its own story, like an

old person recounting their memories, inviting me to relive the time when

it was young, to share its joys and its colours. On visits such as these I have

PREVIOUS PAGES
Pigeonholes filled with sample rolls
in the *Au fil des couleurs* store in Paris.

Shreds of wallpapers by Mauny.

A medley of different patterns, all in blue.

never had anything but happy experiences, and sometimes I am astonished

by the cheerful freshness and lyricism that are exhaled by these tattered

shreds. The patterns are imaginative, the colours strong and simple, and

the papers themselves not as fragile as one might imagine, having survived

the passing centuries with such éclat. Sometimes I have spent long hours

carefully stripping back the layers, so as to piece together an image of a

vanished era. We should not turn a deaf ear to the tales these old and

discarded wallpapers have to tell. They have gems of creativity to reveal

to us; perhaps they can even tell us about our hidden selves?

I OFTEN TEAR NEW AND
RECLAIMED WALLPAPERS
INTO STRIPS AND MIX
THEM TOGETHER TO CREATE

MURAL LANDSCAPES

A reproduction by Mehmet and Dimona Iksel of a late-eighteenth-century tree of life, with its reflection.

I LOVE TO AGE TOO-NEW

    WALLPAPERS BY SPRAYING

    THEM WITH WATER COLOURED

    WITH INK, COFFEE OR TEA

WORN AND FADED WALLPAPERS

Sickly and yellowing though they may be, tiny flowers, clover leaves, buttercups and daisies still seem to scurry all over the walls, like swarms of flies. Their incessant movement makes even the smallest room seem more spacious. Small-patterned wallpaper can be enormously helpful in confined spaces. We should never underestimate the psychological and poetic effects of inanimate objects.

OPPOSITE
I aged this Nobilis wallpaper by tearing it and spraying it with a solution of weak tea.

RIGHT
1 : A little room under the eaves, left as it has always been.
2 : 1937. Sketch Zuber.
3 : c.1830. French frieze.
4 : c.1875. Hand-blocked American domino.

I RUBBED THE DADO

AND WALLPAPER WITH CHALK

To gain the full effect of the luxuriant profusion of the pink flowers on the Sandberg wallpaper in this tiny space, I decided to introduce numerous panels framed with mouldings, even on the ceiling.

SINCE IT'S DIFFICULT

TO FIND SMALL PATTERNS

NOWADAYS, I WORK

Wallpaper with tiny floral patterns can invade walls,
WITH REDUCED
cupboards, drawers, eaves, passages and especially ceilings!
PHOTOCOPIES
This is an infallible way of losing all sense of a room's cramped

dimensions or awkward shape, so that even the most

unpromising space can become a place to dream in.

PREVIOUS PAGES
LEFT TO RIGHT
Sanderson wallpaper
scraped with dry pastel.
Japanese-inspired wallpaper, 1920s.
Cole & Son wallpaper rubbed
with pastel.

RIGHT
1 : 1830. Dufour factory.
2 and 5 : The corridor under the
eaves is papered throughout
with Brunschwig wallpapers.
3, 4, 6 and 7 : Swatches from
Lyon, 1833.

A LEXICON OF PATTERNS

WHICH PATTERNS ARE MOST EXPRESSIVE?

Before choosing a wallpaper, it is essential to realize that you will be living in its company from morning till night and even beyond, as it may well invade your dreams. There are so many patterns to choose from. Nowadays we may choose over-sized motifs and use them sparingly on a single wall of a large room, but you can equally well go to the opposite extreme and choose a tiny pattern that will make as much of a statement through repetition. So make way for cheerful prints! Whether geometric, neo-geometric (protozoa, capsules, pills),

PREVIOUS PAGES
2007. Wallpaper by Initiales.

OPPOSITE
Wallpaper with a pattern of pills and capsules, Graham & Brown.

CENTRE
Detail of an American domino, early nineteenth century.

RIGHT
1 : c.1970. Osborne & Little.
2 and 4 : c.1915. Mauny classic revival.
3 : 2006. Suzy Hoodless for Osborne & Little.

vermiculated or botanical, they have an important part to play in keeping our spirits up. Way ahead of the field, throughout every category and every era, are floral prints – which is hardly surprising, as flowers embody all that is decorative, feminine, beautiful and alive in nature. Floral patterns are reborn every year, to flatter all tastes. Flower motifs are compatible with every period and every style. From the earliest known French wallpaper at the Château de Marcoux, dating from 1650 and sprinkled with lilies, to the most modern designs, flowers reign unchallenged. From delicate rosebuds to blowsy bouquets of full-blown blooms; from camellias, dahlias, peonies and iris to narcissi, lilies-of-the-valley and nasturtiums; from grape hyacinths, petunias and marguerites to campanulas and pinks, tulips and waterlilies, the list of flower prints is endless and all inclusive.

HANDED DOWN FROM GENERATION TO GENERATION, THE SAME MOTIFS ARE CONSTANTLY RENEWED

LEFT
1 : **1906.** Gilbert Breyens for Leroy.
2 : **1902.** Édouard Devillers for Leroy.

LEFT AND OPPOSITE
I pasted strips of this Cole & Son wallpaper, a new edition of a 1950s design, in the fillets of the dado and door panels.

Torn version

FOREVER FLOWERS

Still today, whether geometric, natural or naïve, flowers brighten the daily routine of our urban lifestyle. Pasted on the end wall of a small or narrow room, floral wallpaper will moreover transform it into an enormous garden, boundless and ageless.

YOU CAN HAVE FUN CREATING
COUNTLESS LAYERS OF
FLOWERS, USING STENCILS,
ORIGAMI, KNITTING AND
CROCHET OF ALL KINDS

1978. Wallpaper by Leroy.
Over-drawings of flowers by Philippe Model.

OPPOSITE
Left : Pink coffee bean wallpaper by,
Given Campbell for Brunschwig.
Right: Poster collage by Nathalie Lété for Merci.

LEAVES AND WILD GRASSES

OPEN THE DOOR TO TENDRILS OF IVY
AND LET NATURE IN

A LONE TREE IN SOLITARY SPLENDOUR
OR A MYSTERIOUS FOREST?

Serene and majestic, trees have always been the second most ubiquitous motif, after flowers, in the nature-orientated wallpaper lexicon. Oak or chestnut, acacia or birch, lime or beech, trees offer shelter and nobility at all seasons, their spreading boughs laden with spring blossom or fluttering summer foliage, or frost-etched in wintry splendour or silhouetted by moonlight.

LIGHT FILTERING THROUGH TREE BRANCHES
CREATES AN EFFECT OF
CHIAROSCURO THAT I
CAPTURE BY MEANS OF SUBTLE
COLOUR VARIATIONS

PREVIOUS PAGES
Left and right: The same William Morris wallpaper in two different colour variations. Centre: Panoramic scene by Iksel.

OVERLEAF
Left: Graham & Brown wallpaper with drawing of branches by Philippe Model. Right: Magnetic movable wallpaper by Moove Paper.

A BAMBOO GROVE IN
MAGNETIC WALLPAPER

NOTHING IS MORE RESTFUL
THAN THE GENTLE SPLASHING
AND RIPPLING OF WATER – A
SOOTHING EFFECT THAT MANY
DESIGNERS SEEK TO CAPTURE

RIPPLES AND REFLECTIONS
IN STREAMS AND POOLS

Nature offers us worlds of delight and relaxation, restoring our spirits and refreshing our senses. Plants festoon walls and drape themselves elegantly over trellises, while water – reflecting sun and sky, rippling around waterlilies or gently lapping shells and corals – carries us off into the realm of daydreams. In our imaginations we find ourselves in the lush depths of a Rousseau jungle, with its leafy fronds, monkeys and birds of brilliant plumage.

RIGHT
1 : **1905**. Robert Heidrich for Leroy.
2 : **1930**. René Crevel for ESSEF.
3 : Thibault wallpaper by Besson, crumpled.
4 : **2008**. Pierre Frey.

OPPOSITE
Wallpaper in two different colour versions with fabric by Nobilis.

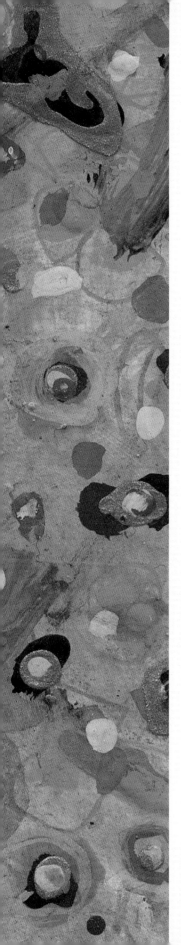

YOU CAN ALMOST HEAR THE
SPARROWS CHIRPING IN
THE CHERRY TREES IN THE
GARDEN, OR CANARIES SINGING
IN THEIR CAGES

OPPOSITE
I coloured in this wallpaper's
hummingbirds and flowers with
watercolours. New edition of a 1930s
design by Décograph, 1970.

LEFT
Design by the American painter Wesley
Johnson, 1994.

RIGHT
1 : 2006. Nina Campbell.
2 : 1917. Desfossé & Karth.
3 : 1958. Leroy.
4 : 1897. Desfossé & Karth.

ELEGANT PARROTS,
       SOLITARY OR IN PAIRS,
       BRIGHTEN THE WALLS,
       BRINGING WITH THEM
       AN AIR OF THE 1920s,
       WHEN THEY WERE
       SO POPULAR

OPPOSITE
Amid a décor of rocks and stones, a
Sandberg wallpaper after an original
from the 1880s.

LEFT
1915. A famous metallic wallpaper
by Georges Barbier for the publisher
Andrés Groult.

RIGHT
1 : c.1915. Wallpaper by Ateliers Groult.
2 : 1905. Ruepp for Leroy.
3 : 2006. Nina Campbell.
4 : 1924. Séguy for Leroy.

FLOWERS AND PLANTS: TRANSFORMATION AND SOPHISTICATION

One of the most fascinating aspects of any motif is the number of ways in which it can be stretched and distorted. Stylized and transformed into geometric patterns, floral motifs offer designers a whole range of fresh inspiration. Leaves become triangular strips, blooms – camellias or dahlias, perhaps – clusters of coloured circles. Symmetrical leaf patterns – a form of stylization with classical credentials, as in the 'acanthus damask' pattern – present opportunities for combining traditional techniques with contrasting colours and textures.

OPPOSITE
Two contrasting designs in vivid pinks on dark brown, both by Tricia Guild.

RIGHT
1, 2 and 4 : Predominantly pink designs characteristic of the mid 1920s.
3 : 1823. Joseph Dufour.

BORDER, FAR LEFT AND RIGHT
Mid-1920s, France.

A CLUTCH OF DAMASK WALLPAPERS

AS CLEAN AND HYGIENIC
AS WALL TILES

The 1870s saw a new discovery: if wallpaper was

waterproofed using a water-repellent varnish, it

could be used in rooms that were susceptible to

damp and condensation. A whole new repertoire

of designs now appeared, inspired by simple

seventeenth-century dominos, Delft tiles or Iznik

tiles from Turkey. These varnished wallpapers

invariably came in a palette of cool, fresh blues,

in striking contrast to the warm brown tones that

otherwise monopolized the period.

ABOVE **1873. Tile wallpaper for 'damp rooms', Desfossé.**

CENTRE **American domino, early nineteenth century.**

OPPOSITE **c.1975. Turkish-inspired tile wallpaper, Besson.**

WALLPAPERS REPRODUCING
MAGNIFICENT IZNIK TILES ARE
STILL AVAILABLE TODAY.
IN A KITCHEN THEY MAY BE
COORDINATED WITH SHELF
BLINDS AND
COMPLEMENTARY CHINA.

OPPOSITE AND CENTRE
A reproduction of traditional Iznik tiles,
with trees, tulips and carnations, Iksel.

RIGHT
c.1845. Long swag of fruit and foliage
including vine and chestnut leaves,
honeysuckle, cherries and strawberries,
a French wallpaper by Wagner.

GOOD VIBRATIONS

Wallpaper has always experimented with designs that are strange, shifting and disturbing. As early as the eighteenth century, multicoloured striped ribbons tied themselves into improbable knots and bows. In the early nineteenth-century, marbled designs rippled and undulated in all directions; and in the 1960s the visual distortions of Op Art triumphed in billowing waves of black and white.

OPPOSITE
c1795. A startlingly original wallpaper testifying to the quest for the new in France under the *Directoire*.

WALLPAPERS OF THE NIGHT

Visual effects based on contrasts are never out of fashion. In 2008, the designers Héléna Ichbiah and Piotr Karczewski, otherwise known as Ich&Kar, conceived the idea of using phosphorescent inks to create wallpapers in two different looks, one for day and the other for night.

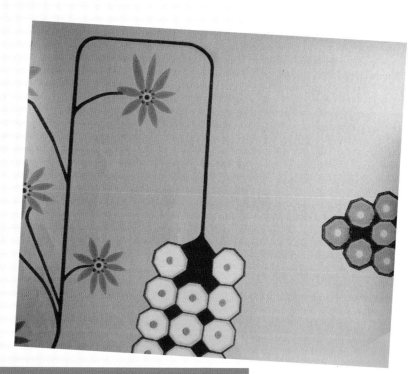

CHANGING OR PHOSPHORESCENT WALLPAPERS OFFER TWO DIFFERENT LOOKS

5/ day

6/ night

7/ day

8/ night

For one of the famous window displays in his Paris antiques showroom, Jacques Hervouet chose Christophe Koziel's Toiletspirit wallpaper for Lutèce. Photo Guy Bouchet.

AN OLD SILVER WALLPAPER INSPIRED AN

IMPROVISED BATHROOM

1900 PALE FLOWERS ON A
SILVERY GUILLOCHÉ BACKGROUND

To show the effect of this grey and silver wallpaper by Given Campbell for Brunschwig, and to demonstrate how metallic reflections can alter our perception of the same design, I asked Marie-Pierre Morel to photograph the salon from two different angles. The harpsichord is also covered with wallpaper, by Cole & Son.

HERE I CHOSE A DIFFERENT COLOUR

SCHEME, INSPIRED BY INDIA

INVITATION TO A VOYAGE, DESTINATION CHINA

The role of wallpaper is not limited to soothing our spirits or offering a pleasant form of relaxation. It can also carry us off to distant lands.

The magic carpet effect begins with a judicious selection of exotic motifs that are redolent of the region in question. That done, it transports us to far-flung places of mystery and glamour: India, perhaps, or China, Japan or Africa, Tahiti or Russia, New York or ...anywhere in the world. The possibilities are limitless.

PREVIOUS PAGES
Left and right: The same metallic paper shown on pages 118–119, this time in vivid tones that create a dramatically different effect.
Centre: 1973. Nobilis.

OPPOSITE
Panels of Osborne & Little and Tricia Guild wallpapers framed in the colours of old Shanghai.

RIGHT
1 : Peony design, late seventeenth century.
2 and 4 : 1832 and 1834. Dufour et Leroy.
3 : 1914. Japanese-inspired English wallpaper.

FAR LEFT AND RIGHT
1830. Border inspired by Chinese silk ribbons, Dufour & Leroy.

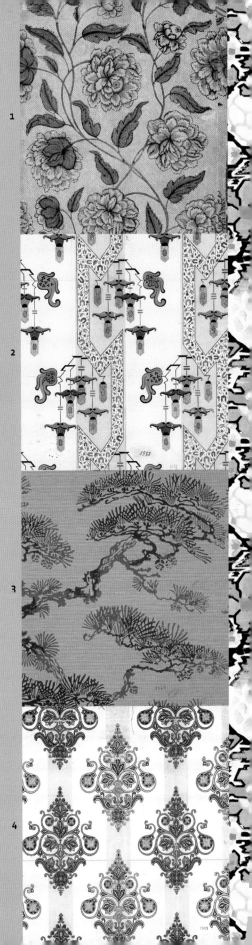

1

3

4

5

124

CHINESE PROCESSION ON A
SEVENTEENTH-CENTURY SCREEN

WALLPAPER CUT-OUTS USED LIKE

THE PANELS OF A KIMONO

AFTER CHINA AND JAPAN
THE ADVENTURE GOES ON

The journey in our imagination to China and Japan has attained classic status. As early as the seventeenth century, motifs based on trees of life, peonies, lanterns and processions of tiny figures through rocky landscapes were firmly rooted in our imaginations. The lure of Africa is more recent. Patterns inspired by canework and basketwork, zebra stripes and dark colours, totems and coffee beans made their appearance in the late eighteenth century. Urban voyages through virtual furturist cityscapes, meanwhile, were foreshadowed in a few geometric building motifs from the mid-nineteenth century, to find full expression in the early twentieth with Cubism and a fascination with structured architectural forms.

OPPOSITE
Wallpapers by Farrow & Ball and Little Green.

RIGHT
1 : Patchwork of Farrow & Ball wallpapers.
2 : 1905. Leroy.
3 : 1830. Dufour et Leroy.
4 : 2000. Montecolino, after an ancient design.

OVERLEAF
Wallpaper by Brunschwig, friezes by Mauny and
Graham & Brown. Centre: Wallpaper by Delta, 1965.

1

2

3

4

JOURNEY TO AFRICA

WITH GEOMETRIC MOTIFS

PAPER COLLAGES

Geometry and paper are good companions. Rolls of wallpaper

can happily accommodate paper cut-outs, improvised

mosaics, random arrangements of squares and labels, and

even post-it notes flitting to and fro (see page 189). I improvise

my collages from scraps of paper and card, including

photocopies in all sizes and cut-out images.

WHAT WOULD I DO WITHOUT THE
COLOUR PHOTOCOPIER? I USE IT

TO REPRODUCE BITS OF PAPER AT

DIFFERENT SCALES IN ORDER TO

CREATE MOVEMENT

RIGHT
1: **1933.** French wallpaper.
2: **c.1915.** French wallpaper.
3: **2006.** AS Créations.
4: **c.1930.** French wallpaper.

OPPOSITE
Collage of paper squares
by Hanna Hansson
for Sandberg,
with cement tiles.

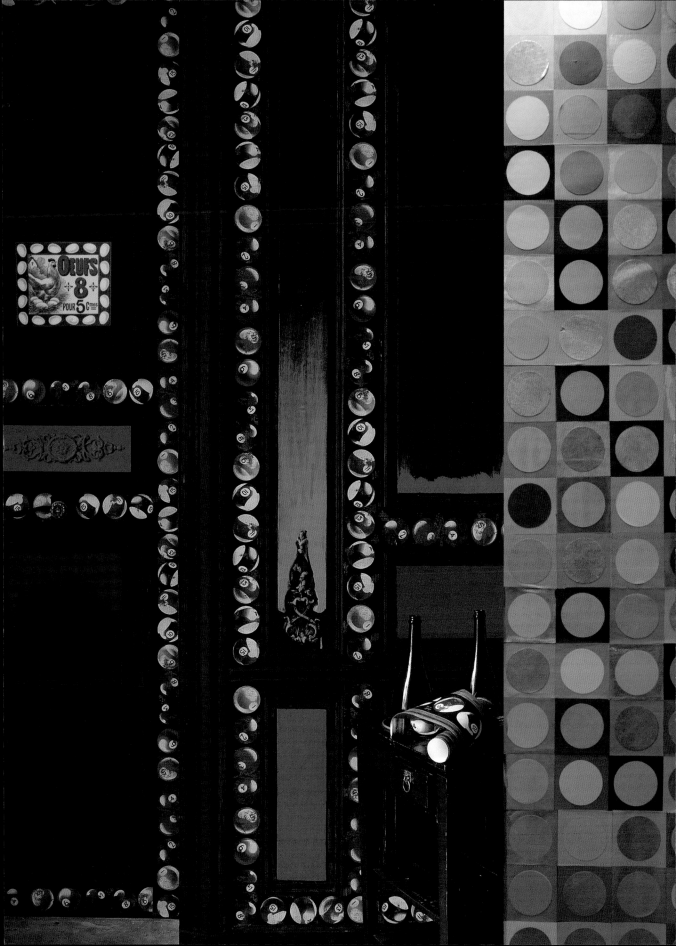

OPPOSITE LEFT
**Frieze with billiard balls,
Initiales.**
OPPOSITE LEFT
**Leather collage by Philippe
Model for Gaiera.**

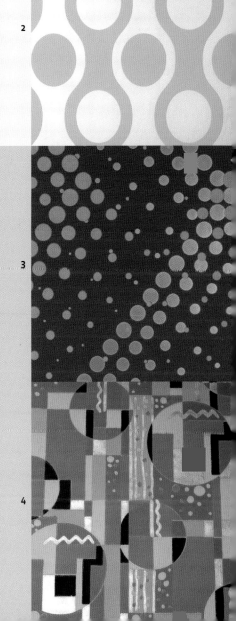

1

2

3

4

I ARRANGE SQUARES OF
LEATHER, ADDING
EMPHASIS WITH
DISCS IN CONTRASTING
COLOURS

INGS AND CIRCLES ON THE MOVE

Geometry is not always a matter of angles and straight lines. Circles, bubbles, balloons, eggs, boules, billiard balls – any number of circular shapes may float across our walls, whether in straight rows, concentric curves or sparkling showers. They also make the perfect complement to other wallpaper patterns, perking them up with their buoyant movement (see pages 38–39).

RIGHT
1 and 2 : **2006**. AS Créations.
3 : **2007**. Grantil.
4 : **1923**. Maurice Gruin.

135

In bedrooms for young children I always recommend patterned wallpaper rather than plain paint finishes. In my mind I remember spending hours as a child making up stories around the images on my walls. Here I cut out rosettes from different colour versions of this wallpaper by Hanna Hansson for Sandberg, so that they float upwards in generous clusters.
OPPOSITE Above: 1948, frieze by Follot. Centre: 1936, France. Below: 1958, frieze by Nobilis.

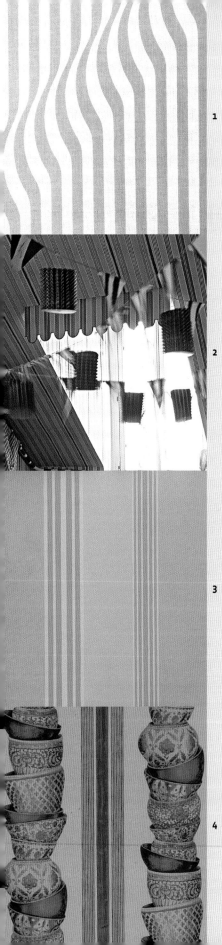

STRIPES CAN BE JAGGED,

OVERPAINTED OR OUT OF

KILTER – JUST AS LONG

AS THEY'RE NOT STRAIGHT

Let's be clear about one thing: immaculately regular striped wallpaper is dull, dull, dull. How much more interesting and attractive are painted stripes, with all their imperfections?

Striped wallpaper should only ever be used in combination with other designs, or if it creates the effect of an awning or open-air *café-dansant* on Bastille Day. Or else choose stripes with an unexpected twist or optical illusion, or that press into service tottering piles of unexpected objects.

LEFT AND ABOVE
1 : **1967.** Inaltéra.
2 : Spirit of Bastille Day, wallpapers by Lewis & Wood.
3 : **c.1955.** Nobilis.
4 : **2008.** Chinese bowls, Pierre Frey.
5 : **1930–1950.** Biscuit tin label.

OPPOSITE
In the bathroom, seven different striped wallpapers by Cole & Son.

1

2

3

TROMPE-L'OEIL TRANSFORMATIONS

Wallpaper has always had fun with trompe-l'oeil effects. One of its best tricks is false library shelves, a perfectly practical illusion that enables you to structure a room and conceal cunningly contrived storage areas.

USED TO LINE THE BACK OF A
NICHE, AT THE FAR END OF A
PASSAGE, ON SCREENS
OR IN CUPBOARDS, TROMPE-L'OEIL
EFFECTS CREATE SPACE AND
PERSPECTIVES

LEFT
1 : **1911**. Leroy.
2 : **1967**. Société française du papier peint.
3 : **1953**. Piero Fornasetti for Cole & Son.
4 : **1904**. Leroy.

OPPOSITE
In the bona fide library, I have added screens papered with false bookshelves, Brunschwig, new edition of a 1950s design.

4

LIKE COLOURS, PATTERNS COME
ALIVE WHEN BROUGHT
FACE TO FACE.
ECHOING OR CONTRASTING,
EVERY ONE CREATES A
DIFFERENT ATMOSPHERE

Two different wallpapers can transform a room

in two very different ways. The same is true of

two different shades of the same pattern, or

two variations of a single motif. Some shades

generate feelings that are diametrically

opposed to others: when I create colour ranges,

I am often astonished by the variety of

ambiences they create.

Around the same *oeil-de-boeuf*
window I used first of all a black
and cream Little Green wallpaper,
then a new romantic prototype of
my own design.

EVERY ROOM HAS ITS INDIVIDUAL CHARACTER, ITS OWN PERSONALITY.

I ALWAYS TAKE TIME TO LIVE IN THEM AND GET

TO KNOW THEM BEFORE WORKING

OUT WHAT CHANGES TO MAKE.

WHERE?

HOW?

PREVIOUS PAGES
In the low-ceilinged bedroom, I have
hung the walls and ceiling with
Suzy Hoodless wallpapers for Osborne &
Little and vintage 1970s wallapers.

THERE ARE NO SET RULES

I'm not going to tell you that you shouldn't use wallpaper on just one wall of

a room, or the back of a shelved alcove, or a large sliding door, or one wall of

a straight flight of stairs … You know all about how wallpaper is used in

contemporary design. Every wallpaper retailer, every hypermarket sales area

and every television makeover show has told you more than you could ever

need to know.

BUT WE SHOULD RESPECT A
ROOM'S CHARACTER

What I would like to say is that, for me, a room is like a person, with its own
character, faults and personality. It is what it is. It may be like a petite young
girl, graceful in ballet pumps, or like a tall, statuesque woman who is even
more striking in high heels. Don't be afraid to paper the ceiling of a low room
(see previous pages) and to use floor cushions and low sofas. It will make it
even cosier and more comfortable, even more itself. By the same token, a
repeating vertical pattern in a lofty-ceilinged room will make the walls seem
even higher. Every house has its own proportions: let's celebrate them!

CENTRE AND OPPOSITE
Wallpaper with a pattern of television
sets in relief, by Rasch, 2002, exaggerates
the height of already lofty walls.
Chandelier by Pierre Griperay.

PREVIOUS PAGES
Kinetic patterns by Sedim-
Marburg, Lutèce and Cole &
Son and a papered bicycle
infuse concrete with life.
Centre top: Wallpaper
publishers' stand at the Paris
trade fair, 1953.

OPPOSITE
A village in felt, cork,
tartan, snakeskin and and
rubber tyre by Antoine &
Manuel, masters of the art
of patchwork.

THE ART OF PATCHWORK

Patchwork helps me in the design process. Just

as you can like a number of different papers, so

you can decide which ones to buy by choosing

colours or patterns: one roll like this, one roll like

that ... Then it's time to cut them up, mix them

all together, arrange them. With a little quiet

concentration, it soon falls into place. Time for

the scissors! In the following pages I have chosen

examples of different types of patchwork, around

a theme, a colour or a technique. Your turn!

PATCHWORK, IT SEEMS TO ME, IS NOT ONLY EASY
BUT ALSO DISCRIMINATING, AS
EVERY MOTIF WHEN CUT OUT IS SO
MUCH MORE INTERESTING, AND NO
LONGER A SINGLE DOMINANT PRESENCE
OF WHICH YOU MIGHT EASILY TIRE

I PICKED WHITE WALLPAPERS

WITH BLACK LINE DRAWINGS

THAT I CAN COLOUR IN USING FELT-TIP PENS

VARIATIONS ON BLACK OR

VERY DARK BACKGROUNDS

Brightly coloured wallpapers with naïve motifs, cut like boards, evoke central European folk art, traditional flower festivals and the swaying and jolting of gipsy caravans.

ONCE YOUR PATTERNS ARE SORTED, BY COLOUR, SHAPE OR SPIRIT, WORK ON THE PATCHWORK CAN BEGIN

PREVIOUS PAGES
Left: Patchwork of papers by Little Green, Rasch, Zuber. Centre: Wallpaper by Sandberg, frieze by Mauny.
Right: The same frieze with wallpaper by Eric Valéro for Nobilis.

OPPOSITE
I transformed the boards of the cabin using wallpapers by Cole & Son, Little Green and Nobilis, along with vintage 1960s wallpapers and wrapping paper.

THE WARMTH OF A PATCHWORK QUILT IN PAPER

A crossover between a traditional Provençal patchworkquilt, or *boutil*, and a faux patchwork on the walls. Forget needles and threads and wadding: simply cut out the paper patches and glue them on the wall in your chosen pattern. [1]

EVERY NOW AND THEN I THROW A PATCHWORK
PAPER PARTY, WHERE ALL
THE GUESTS BRING
SWATCHES THAT THEY CUT
OUT AND STICK DOWN AS THEY
LIKE, BEFORE CELEBRATING
OUR JOINT CREATION

OPPOSITE AND RIGHT
Patchwork using wallpapers
by William Morris, Cole & Son,
Osborne & Little and Sandberg.

OPPOSITE
1 and 2 : Hand-blocked swatches from the 1830s.

2

Foppot - Paris

I used a variety of Cole & Son and Little Green wallpapers in shades of grey to pick out the vertical wooden glazing bars in the factory.

I NEVER ATTEMPT TO HIDE ANY
LOPSIDEDNESS IN THE
CUTTING OR PASTING
OF STRIPS, BOARDS OR
BANDS: IT IS THESE SPONTANEOUS
IRREGULARITIES THAT CREATE MOVEMENT

SCISSORS OR SAW?

Cutting irregular strips from a variety of wallpapers and arranging them like floorboards is hugely satisfying, as the unexpected juxtapositions make the patterns sing.

LEFT
René Litt's numerous designs are all imbued with joyous creativity. 1953, René Litt.

CENTRE
I had fun juxtaposing strips of different designs by René Litt from the years 1953 to 1955.

OPPOSITE
Wallapers by Little Green, Osborne & Little and Sandberg creating an effect of old boards, with a felt feather rug by Philippe Model.

I ADORE RIPPING WALLPAPER.

HERE I SET ABOUT IT WITH A HAMMER,

LIKE A ROCK

PREVIOUS PAGES: Fornasetti malachite wallpaper for Osborne. Right: 2003, Osborne and Little.
RIGHT AND OPPOSITE: Wallpaper in wide strips with stepped cut-outs lends structure to an otherwise featureless space. Little Green.

THE KITCHEN IS RESPLENDENT WITH LABELS

FROM AMERICAN FRUIT CRATES

ALTERNATIVE

WALLPAPERS

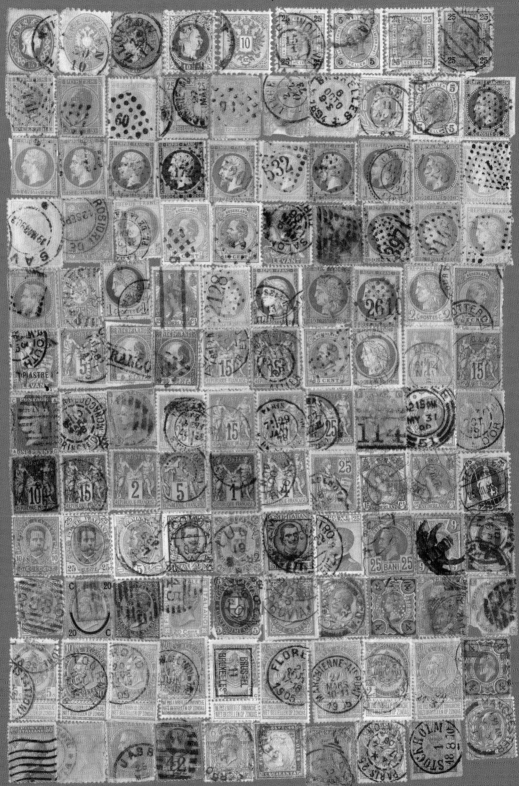

MY COLLECTIONS OF MAGAZINE

COVERS AND CARDS MAKE

KALEIDOSCOPIC WALL COVERINGS

An intrepid traveller ponders his next expedition.

Virtually the whole of Europe is here.

We are all surrounded by a treasure trove of potential alternative wallpapers

waiting to be discovered. Newspapers, postcards, tickets, labels, maps,

matchboxes, postage stamps – the list of everyday paper ephemera that can

I PAPERED THE PANELLING

be transformed on our walls is endless. I looked for road maps in my local

TO CREATE MY OWN VERSION

bookshop. 'For which country?' the bookseller enquired. 'No idea,' I replied,

OF A MAP ROOM OF THE

'Which are the cheapest?' On that occasion I returned home clutching maps

SIXTEENTH

of Belgium and Germany, and set to work. Or of course you could paper your

OR SEVENTEENTH CENTURY

walls with maps of your favourite places. The hanging technique is exactly

the same as for rolls of wallpaper.

PREVIOUS PAGE
Carpet, La Photofactory, background paper, René Kormann.

OPPOSITE AND ABOVE
Road maps, ironed, cut up and pasted on the panelling.

Green labels in the bathroom.

CRUMPLED FRUIT WRAPPERS

I have always wondered – with the wonder you reserve for insignificant things and vanished folk crafts – at the rustling paper wrappers used to protect mandarins. In Morocco, Spain and Italy, these scraps of tissue paper illustrated with naïve images make perfect wrappings, either crumpled or twisted, for citrus fruit and even pears. I felt very honoured when some friends gave me their magnificent collection. I loved using them – some cut up, others left whole – in this book.

LEFT
Coloured paper bands
for ham and sausage.

RIGHT
Labels from French
regional charcuterie.

OPPOSITE
Moroccan labels and Russian
flour boxes in the kitchen.

SIROP
DE GRAND LUXE
CITRON
PUR SUCRE

DISTILLERIE DU PERSAN
14. Gde Rue St Just
MARSEILLE

5

OPPOSITE
My vision of cut-out Spanish labels
in shades of blue.
1 : c.1945. Paul Gruin for Le Mardelé.
2, 4 and 5 : Bottle labels.
3 : 1924. French wallpaper.

ABOVE
Crumpled tissue paper softly reflects the light.

RIGHT
1888. Leroy.

FRUIT BAGS

Simply keep the brown paper bags in which market stall holders sell their fruit. Mixed up and pasted on a brown wall, they create an atmosphere of fruity cheerfulness.

WHENEVER I SHOP IN LITTLE LOCAL MARKETS IN FRANCE OR ITALY, I ALWAYS LOOK OUT FOR PRETTY RETRO PAPER BAGS TO PUT ON THE WALLS ON MY RETURN

You have to eat a lot of fruit and vegetables to create a décor like this.

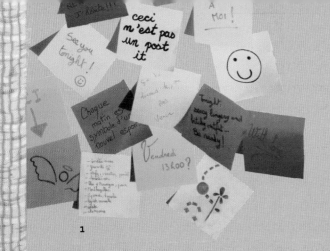

1

2

IN CONCLUSION

Patterns of every kind – whether on paper ephemera or swatches, whether

pretty and floral or geometric and contemporary – share the great virtue of

soothing away the tensions and anxieties of our hectic lifestyles. In addition

to creating a general impression and ambience when viewed from a distance,

PAGE AFTER PAGE, I HAVE

wallpapers also draw us in, encouraging us to discover every last detail of

FALLEN FOR EVERY

their motifs, to relish the time we spend in their company. We can all imagine

SWATCH AND SAMPLE

having a room that constantly surprises and refreshes us, recharging our

batteries. All we have to do is work out the motifs, styles and periods that

genuinely suit us, that truly touch our feelings. This emotional connection

is a deep one, and it may bear no relation to the latest trends – but no one

one will hold it against us if through wallpaper we can come to a deeper

understanding of our own selves.

3

1 : **2006**. Post-it note wallpaper, Myrine Créations.
2 : **c.1855**. Quilted damask wallpaper, Zuber.
3 : **1954**. René Litt.
4 : **c.1775**. Provincial French domino.

4

16 / 1-3-7-9-11: 1787, designs for
waistcoats
2-8: c.1785, trees of life, China
4: 2008, Pierre Frey, eighteenth-century
archive
5: c.1775, screen, China
6: Brunschwig, eighteenth-century
archive
10: 1835, Dufour & Leroy

19 / 1-4-5: Mauny, late eighteenth-
century
2-3-6-7: c.1785, wallpapers, Paris
8: Brunschwig, c.1785

20 / 1: 1794, palmettes, wallpaper, Paris
2: 1835, Dauptain, eighteenth-century
3: bands of palmettes, Brunschwig,
after a wallpaper of c.1790
4: c.1800, Audouin for Legrand
5-6: Mauny, c.1790
7-8: 1800, Verthier for Legrand
9: c.1790, design for Réveillon, Paris

26-27 / 1-2-3-5-6-7: c.1818, flock
wallpapers by Zuber
4: c.1820, sepia panoramic scene by Zuber

28-29 / 1-3-4-15-24: 1831, Collection
Maeght
2-19: 1814, French manufacture
5-6-8-21: c.1820, Joseph Dufour
7-16-17: 1828, Zuber
9-12: c.1825, Nerii, Paris
10-20: 1825, Dufour & Leroy
11: c.1820, Martin factory
13-14-18-23: c.1825, borders
22: Mauny, after an original of 1820

32-33 / Decor: wallpaper, Zoffany,
fabrics, Pierre Frey, hats, Philippe Model.
1: c.1855, Charles Bandon
2-5-7-8: c.1850, Jean Broc
3-9-12: c.1845, Jules Riottot
4-10: 1849, Wagner factory
6: 1861, Zuber
11: 1833, Dufour & Leroy
36-37 / Decor: dado,

Sandberg. Tall panelling,
revarnished, Graham & Brown
1-13: 1790, designs for waistcoats
2-5-7-10-16: 1895–1907, Leroy
3: 1868 Desfossé
4-12: 1868, Collection Maeght
6: c.1890 Dumas
8: c.1875, sunrays and clouds
9: c.1810, decor, German design
11: 2005, Atelier Mériguet-Versrrère
14: 1810, Joseph Dufour
15: 1870, Charles Balin

38-39 / Decors page 39: 1880,
patchworks of William Morris
wallpapers
1-5-6-7-8: 1898, wallpapers by Leroy
2: 1904, Leroy
3: 2005, Neisha Crosland
4: 1898, Christopher Dresser
9: 1895, Joseph Petitjean
10: 1896, Hector Guimard for
Le Mardelé

40 / 1-2-4-6-8-10-11: c.1925, Follot
3: 1915-1920, Lloyd
5: 1915-1920, Gampert
7-12: 1915-1920, d'Espagnat for Groult
9: c.1910, French frieze

48-49 / 1: 1947, Léonor Fini for ESSEF
2: c.1937, France
3: c.1930, Benedictus
4: 2006, Montecolino
5: 1912, Atelier Martine
6-7: 1928, Primavéra
8: 1947, Gilbert Poillerat

50-51 / Decor: Éric Valéro for Nobilis
1: 1958, Inaltéra
2: 2006, Cole & Son
3: 1950, Charles Colin for Follot
4: 1949, Nobilis
5: 1952, design for Zuber
6: 1955, René Litt for Décofrance
7: 1953, René Litt for Zuber
80-81 / Decors: page 80, Hanna
Hansson wallpaper for Sandberg,

page 81, paintwork, wallpapers and
tiles by Emery & Cie.
1-2: 2006, Collection Feuillages
3: 1925, Follot
4: 1968, Zuber

84-85 / 1-3: 2006, Graham & Brown
2: Sandberg, from an eighteenth-century
original
4: 2004, Larsen
5: 2007, Initiales
6-7-8-10: 2005, Cole & Son
9: 2007, Rasch
11: 2007, Myrine Créations
12: 2007, Jean-Charles de Castelbajac
13: 1934, Follot
14: 2007, Osborne & Little

88-89 / Centre, floral column: 1860,
Délicourt
1: c.1820, Joseph Dufour
2: 1855, Desfossé
3: Mauny, after a wallpaper of c.1815
4: c.1875, France
5-9-14: c.1785, French latticework designs
6: nineteenth-century design after a
seventeenth-century original
7: Iksel, after Jacquemart, 1791
8: c.1800, French manufacture
10: 1867, border, Paris
11: 1828, Zuber
12-13-15: c.1960, Nobilis
16: c.1830, France

92-93 / Decor, page 92, left:
2008, Pierre Frey, page 92, right: 2005,
Cole & Son
1-5: c.1912, France
2-7: Iksel, after a nineteenth-century
original
3: 2003: Manuel Canovas
4-9: 2005, Initiales
6: 1862, Zuber
8: Zoffany, from an original of c.1790
10: 2007, Lutèce
11: 2007, Sandberg
12: 2007, Les Munchausen

Creative Director: **Philippe Model**
Design and Art Director: **Gaëlle Chartier**
Photogravure and montages: **Michel Sixou**
Editorial Director: **Nathalie Bailleux**

ACKNOWLEDEMENTS

My thanks go to Gaëlle Chartier, who was such a pleasure to work with; to Véronique de la Hougue, gifted head of the wallpaper department at the Musée des Arts Décoratifs, who was of great assistance to me; to Béatrice Salmon, head curator; to the Bibliothèque Forney, where Frédéric Casiot, curator, Dominique Deangeli-Cayol and Sylvie Pitoiset, heads of wallpaper and advertising material, were always warm and helpful; to Philippe de Fabry, at the Musée du Papier Peint at Rixheim; to Maryse Gourmand, my very patient assistant; to Carole Texier, Franck Halard of Au fil des couleurs, Édith, Nathalie, Marianne and Laurent; to Christelle de Montbel and Maud Olivier of the Association A3P, who responded to my questions with such good humour; to Gisèle Chalais of Zuber, who opened up the firm's archives to me; to Pierre-Yves Bonnet, great specialist in antique wallpapers; to Jean-Baptiste Martin, antique dealer and restorer and Jacques Hervouet. To Catherine Gamard of Agence Mires, Valentina Russino and Fabrice Uzan of Gambino, Florence Maeght, Christine Model-Baker, Marie-Louise Fort, Dominique Giraud, Anne-Sophie d'Amiens, Pilar Saltini, Myriam and Séverin Laface, Atelier Mériguet-Carrère, the Photofactory, de Gournay of London, Emery & Cie, Nobilis and Élisabeth Pollock, Patrick and Lorraine Frey, La Galerie Sentou, and finally to Michel Sixou, Patricia Perdrizet and the entire team at Un sourire de toi!

Published in the UK by Scriptum Editions
An imprint of Co & Bear Productions (UK) Ltd
www.scriptumeditions.co.uk
Distributed by Thames & Hudson
Translation © Co & Bear Productions (UK) Ltd, 2010
Translation by Barbara Mellor

10 9 8 7 6 5 4 3 2 1
ISBN: 978–1–902686–72–1
Printed in China

© Editions du Chêne-Hachette Livre, 2010 in the original work.
First published, in French, by
Editions du Chêne-Hachette Livre, 2009
Original Title: *Les Papiers Peints: Arts Décoratifs*

© CREDITS

Photographs of decors are by Marie-Pierre Morel, except:
pages 9, 55, 88 centre (Palazzo Altemps, Rome, su concessione del Ministero per i Beni e le Attività Culturali – Soprintendenza Speciale per i Beni Archeologici di Roma), 112–115, 126, 136, 144–147, 154, 164, 183 and 184 © Joël Laiter,
page 21 © Jean-Baptiste Martin,
page 30 © Jean-François Jaussaud,
pages 56–58 © Luc Boegly,
pages 67 and 153 © Christian Bouvier,
page 110 © Guy Bouchet,
page 109 far right © Erwan Frotin.

Photographs of wallpaper swatches from the Musée des Arts Décoratifs on pages 1, 13, 19, 20,31, 32, 36, 38, 45, 48, 49, 60, 67, 71, 78, 88 à 90, 95, 97, 99, 100, 102, 109, 111, 117,123, 124, 127, 131, 137, 138, 140, 152, 153, 157, 161, 165, 168, 184, 188, 189 and 192 are by Jean Tholance © Arts décoratifs/Jean Tholance, all rights reserved.